Baker of Tarifa

Baker of Tarifa

Poems by

Shadab Zeest Hashmi

Cover design & Section art by Azfar Najmi
Window image by Amitai Touval

Poetic Matrix Press
P.O. Box 1223
Madera, CA 93639
www.poeticmatrix.com

For Yaseen, Yousuf, Yousha

And For Shameem
who has wandered through the geography and history
of Al Andalus with me, navigating all manner of emotive
terrain – I could not ask for a more insightful, spirited
and supportive companion.

Acknowledgements

My deepest thanks to Eleanor Wilner for guiding me in crucial ways, to Sam Hamill for encouraging me to persevere through the roughest part of this journey, to Tarik and Julia Banzi of the *Al Andalus Ensemble* whose music inspired this work. Thanks to Brandon Cesmat for including poems from this manuscript in his film *Cruzando Lineas: Crossing Lines*, and to the following publications where some of these poems first appeared:

Pakistani Literature
The Cortland Review
Poetry International
San Diego Poetry Annual
Pakistaniyaat: A Journal of Pakistan Studies

Finally, my gratitude to both my parents whose enthusiasm has given this work the energy it needed, and whose essence is very much a part of this book.

— Shadab Zeest

Contents

Lambent

Biography

Of the two bestirred, sleepless nights, the first was spent in Cordoba's Juderia, yards away from the Mezquita-Catedral where the streets are narrow as capillaries. And the second was in the Alhamra where my room was a whisper away from the *Rauda*, the royal graveyard of the Nasrids. The ghosts of Al Andalus have clung ever since.

And so windows crack open. Under streetlights, ancient faces are embedded in pillars. Sketched in rust they bleed into each other. These ghosts of Al Andalus come on rich wafts of tannin ink and pomegranate pulp, or poised between *oud* strings – vibrato of a dream. They leap from a basin of mercury to the high, filigreed domes...

Some have a furtive way of surfacing in a note of the *ney* flute, slipping ever so lightly into the seam joining two breaths, while others place themselves stubbornly on my patio ledge in California, legs dangling, refusing to leave until I hear them out.

They are scribes and stonemasons, merchants, seamstresses, philosophers, gardeners and governors. They plant, they write books. They build, and make bread. One of them, a child known as Yusuf, Yosef and Joseph appears out of nowhere. Not found in history books, he is among the last fortunate ones to be cherished by the people of the three Abrahamic faiths. His home, Al Andalus, has seen a fruition great enough to inspire other golden ages in other places. But Al Andalus itself will fall, nearly a millennium after its birth. When it does, the Andalusi Muslims, Jews and Christians will part ways in bitterness. Yusuf, like the prophet in the Torah, the Bible and the Quran, will see the end in a dream. Three hundred years later, the end will come.

These ghosts, like fireflies, glow only for an instant. I have come to catch their light—

Al Andalus, Spain 711 – 1492

Baker of Tarifa

Coals Left Over
from Breakfast
Will be Enough

Alcazar in a Dream

A wide window
drawn in charcoal on the palace wall

for peasants to hop across
meet the geometricians

Painted whisper glass
buds to overhang

Converse
with fruit bats

Then a pendant
of light swung

& spun itself a shadow helix

O darting
eclipse
They once called you dove

And was there not some sweet

bread
in your bill?

The dough lies dreaming
Pregnant
and smooth in an earthen basin
It is summer and the soap white curtains
are exhaling like sails

There is far away laughter
And a pulse nearby
in oil
semolina

She catches the pulse
the imprint of fate-lines

It is the summer
Of barley   white flour   spiced honey lavender sourdough
From the houses of Jewish leather merchants
Christian boatmen singers
Muslim botanists

Held by a mother
with kohl-lined eyes

Bread
for apricot-skinned children

Baker of Tarifa

Coals left over from breakfast
will be enough

You'll need a cup of crushed
almonds
(pistachios cost more than a bottle
of Syrian perfume these days
so do without)
brown sugar and plenty of butter

Also an eye-cup of rosewater
for the filling
Muqawwara means arena
Cut the bread
neatly in that shape

Take care the dough has been softened
with fresh milk

Sing
what your mother sang
while you fry the bread

The Confectioners' District in Sevilla: Bakers Chant

The river Sweets in its spine	Sweets in its spine	Gold in mouth
The river	Shivering before dawn	Honeycomb
	Simmering alchemy	Gold's honey boiling
	Shivering	Shivering before dawn
Before dawn *The confectioners* awaken The confectioners awaken	To different gods	Same sugar
	From orange blossom Blossom	Dreams
	Figs Pomegranates	Cream
	Promises Honey become word	Of milk and honey
The river stirs	Word become vapor	Rises
The ovens heat up	The dough rises The dough rises	The dough rises The dough rises
The sun rises	Honey river boils over Heaven and Hell	Hell and Heaven
The sun rises	On the patisseries	The bakeries
Sugar dust rises	In places of worship Same God Different places	Different places Same God
Sugar dust settles	All scores	

A Scribe
is Visited by a Jinni
in a Sugarcane Field

When their eyes locked
she saw paper

acres
of sweet milled paper

The field had melted
from green to copper
pulp to gauze

A hush was falling

She bolted from the gaze
Upset her inkpot

A rich black
soaked
through the chewed up cane
stain of cynosure
on the day's lost wages

Europe's First Palm

The fronds:
concentrically
arranged laughter

A single palm
makes a grove of ghazals

Green windows open
out to Rusafa

My Husband Brings
a "Poet's Rabab"
From Abroad

Neither boat nor pear shaped
and I doubt the parchment
is sheepskin

and it caused such bickering

until you
slid the bow
and it was as if
I was swimming across seven lulled seas

It now leans on the west wall
pouring into my manuscript

bubbling
with the eastern Mulberry it came from
Meandering silk
Its mother tongue

A Halva Vendor
Bemoans a Legendary Calligrapher

I see you about town
trying on sandals
mumbling
but the doves laughed

over and over
Cheeks puffed with
fig halva

You don't know your name
Haven't changed your shirt in days
An egret stretches
from end to end of your nebula

I have studied your delicate strokes
Your volumes
fill the caliph's library

Here
Try these pistachios
in hot syrup
Yes
You need decent shoes
for the court in Cairo.

Marzipan Roses
in the Monastery

Saffron in the paste
gives it the color
of the horizon
in summer

Decide on an odd
number of petals

Roll out small
disks of marzipan
Curl the edges
with your thumb and forefinger

Press them into a cone
(shaped like a
a friar's nose)

Set some apart
for ants to smuggle

Give thanks

Wallada's Last Poem for Ibn Zaydun

My rasp
is turned to chalk
Your gushing refrain
wrung dry

a warbler
fills our plaster
ears
with news

a beehive
stirs
beneath the whitewash

A Prince
Makes his Choice

I walked past the walrus ivory
chessmen
and the deer bone

My tutors
sat complaining about the hour

but none of the ladies
had killed the king yet

The courtiers were
beginning to doze off
I settled at the table
opposite a girl
hooded and quick

The rock crystal chessmen
moved like magic
in her butterball hands

Last Day
At the School of Needlework

I have autumn grapes
for fingertips
The girls teased

It is raining now
as it so often did
when we sewed golden fringed
tablecloths for Christmas

They said I'm pale as onion-skin

I am kissing them goodbye
as they pass needles through sheer
sleeves and purple

Yes the purple
velvet
cut in my dimensions

An over-gown
for a seamstress

the day before she weds a prince

A Game of Six, Deuce and Ace

It's the old
quarrel between faith and reason

One in a faded pomegranate
gown and the other

more dapper
wearing a slate caftan
hair combed back

They throw the dice
They throw the dice

Divorce

The dove's necklace hangs
on the door of the courthouse

Pastry and love letters
crumble

Look,
an infantry
of scrawling ants!

Zoraya the Cartographer
Finds the Child

*[Long after Yusuf had become a young man, he would ask
Zoraya to tell the story of how she came to be his mother.]*

Now the walls thick with time
Heavy with the sap the low lyre of sleep
Encroached on my pile of work
(maps to be copied onto parchment all night)
And I dreamt of copper sands clean-
      slate blue starlight

Until the sun cracked through the skin
Of the tower
      hanging a great light in the window

There under the tree shaped like a pilgrim-flask
you were climbing out of a bucket of wild herbs
while the mule and his master slept
surrounded by urns of flax
China hemp and God knows what

I saw your white tunic getting caught in brambles
as you made for the edge of the river
      Like one gone mad
I ran across the Roman bridge
with no sandals or shawl

And you came to my arms as if you had always been mine
Your long hair smelling of aniseed
and sugarcane husk
Your small hands muddy and specked with scratches
behind which I saw lines most beautiful
No map of flower or bird-shaped
land could compare

No land could compare
the seedless dirt beneath my feet
Yusuf was the only word you spoke
And I called you Yusuf the light of my eyes

Samuel the Physician Becomes a Father
And Calls the Child Yosef

The night was shoveling its coal
sighing as darkness licked
my work table
piled with seeds
crushed citron leaves
twigs of olive and thyme
There were canisters of oils
Green walnuts
Bottles of ink and lime shrubs

I should have been happy
with all this life crowding my house
as I lit the candles
dusk pouring thickly over my roof

But happiness grows in the beams
of your eyes alone
It grows
And gives shade

You gaze
as if you have always been mine

That day
when Zoraya the Berber map-maker
brought you scratched by thorns and splinters
that day God made you my son

Maria de La Luz Finds Joseph
the Book Merchant

I am given to looking back
as I walk with the other washer-women
A longing to read words
strung like jeweled ships

comes over me

The writing follows
me from the mosque to the synagogue
across the river
back to the marketplace

I color street corners blue
erasing ink
off the nobles' shirts
dipping them in rose-water

Today
Joseph the book merchant with the open face
taught me how a book is bound
in return for his shirt

My name he says means light
so he read to me about planets
catching starlight
And then he shared
partridge in cumin and yogurt

His name means
the interpreter of dreams

Yusuf Recalls the Day
his Father's Donkey Ran Away

Was it the oak down by the *maristan*
you collected wild anis after church
and I measured and cut parchment
where Samuel's donkey once broke loose from the tree
And ran away with the cart!
What a parade
with everyone trying to stop him!
Someone even begged:
"My brother!" he said "stop!"
Our stuff clattered,
flour canisters rolling,
a dozen tambourines
striking against salt jars and fishing poles
beaded pillows shimmering in the sun
like it was somebody's wedding party!

Invasion

Had you not become a stranger
so many times
I would have considered the moon
my own raw self, slipping out of the impossible
blue mist, dropping into your gaze whole.

You could be the sinewy branches that reach
for me all four seasons. All hundred
and one changing parts
of each season, we could dominate
the avenue between earth and sky.

You on the other side
of this war now

Come unwrap your true voice and say it. Say
that it killed you as many times
when lightning cracked between us,
say the horizon seemed to slink away
into that distant blade-star
leaving you
with the same gash as mine. Say
that you scarred a red scar
when I was cut.

And say the moon, it fell on you
like a bitter fruit.

The End of the War

I entered the city gates in a blind-fold
led by nothing but the summer drift
of fairy-roses
the secret musk of books

How the market puffed up
with flags and shrouds
For a few drachmas
I bought a shroud for my sword
and buried it
under the Bitter-Almond tree

Next I bought a pail of azaleas
a lamp and a saffron mantilla

wrapped in which all night
I watched ink
silently make sparrows
out of its dormant language

Morning broke on the page
I was reading
And I let words fall
into tightly woven nests

And I let illumination
be the song

Yusuf Sees the Ghost
Of the Last Queen of Al Andalus

She dragged empty cradles
into the Alpujarras
while bells
rang with the sound of cannons

Neither Feasting
nor fasting was allowed

The house was filled
with pine nuts
soft cheese
and mint juice
It was as if we never ate

She said to bring the *muezzin*
to her child's ear
She said to draw
the curtains
on *Eid* day

Window for Four Voices

The Window was square	equal on all sides	Equal	On all sides
Equal	In an unjust Whole	Whole	Whole
It was a square window	with roots that reached emerald recesses	Seeking	Energy From the blood of garnets
It was a butterfly window	Symmetrical	Symmetrical	And still
It grew between a Redwood and a pale Chinar	Painted orange for warmth		
It was a flying window A comfort at dusk		Painted purple for bruises	The window was equal on all sides
It was a cool window the breeze not blowing But resting on it	Painted black for peace.		
The window was a nest. It was a lute, a harp.	A tambourine tambourine	A tambourine tambourine	A tambourine tambourine
It was a soft window			painted blue for rain.

It cracked through			
	Turquoise	And tourmaline	It swam in lava
It was a green window And when the world sank for the last time Closing in on itself The window remained open *On all sides*	fluid	And forgiving	
	Square *On all sides*	Equal *On all sides*	*On all sides*

27

Because
My Heart
Became a Kiln

Montage

The Andalusian
is known for sensitivity and intelligence.

A Christian Chronicler writes of Muslims:
"The handsomest among them
was as black as the cooking pot."

Adafina is a cooking pot
used by Jews. It is buried
in embers on Friday night.
The meal is ready
the next day.

On Friday
Muslims are advised
to take the long way home
after prayer
so they can greet neighbors.

Christians
must love their neighbor
as themselves.

Adafina
comes from "dufn" or "buried" in Arabic.

The Andalusian is often
drawn with black pigment.

Arabic is a Semitic language.

Burnt bones were
used to make black.

The Andalusian is mostly gray
and rarely has a pearl,
buckskin or chestnut
coat.

The highest commandment
For Jews, Muslims and Christians:
Love God with all your heart, soul
And mind.

The Andalusian is prized
as a war horse.

Window of the Oratory

I was reading in lamplight
by the oratory
of the sleepless one
when the galloping was heard

We left our bread in the *furn*
Cinnamon half-ground
Pepper oil or wheat flour or ink
on our fingers and dogs barking

Hooves slapped the mud
"Al Ghalib!" I was the first to shout
"Al Ahmer!"

Spring rain fell
on the terra cotta roofs
ivory parsnips
old carob trees

Head bare
His battle turban overturned
collected rain
as if it were mercy falling:
drachmas from our fields
And looms

Our ovens were hot
our ink wet
while in Sevilla's battleground
rain was making rafts of the dead

So near death so near death
Fevered
he spoke to the fragrant mud
That last cover to our mortal
helplessness

"La Ghalib Illa Allah"
"God alone is the victor"
In the distance the Sierra Nevada
Drank
And drank his words

Diary of A Wartime Chef

Only winter berries
Wild mushrooms and each of us
half the man he came

No more of heroes
Instead they want to hear
advice:
Always keep the mortar clean

Recipes:
Before frying in sweet oil,
slash and coat the eggplants
with a mixture of egg whites, pepper,
cilantro juice, murri and powdered lavender.
Serve hot
with segments of citrus.

They fall asleep
Between bread and entrée
and more advice:
Use medium sized eggplants

They lay there
emaciated

Remember to fill the cuts with salt
to remove bitterness .

Plague Prayers

O coniferous center
We plead, we whisper into your ever-pardoning ear

Here, a hymn radiating
from a diaphragm of solid gold

Here, a goat sacrificed in your name
Fists, fits, shame.

Here, I bow, I weep,
I sweep this most exquisite temple

Lord, forgive us
For carrying the cots of unbelievers
for thinking the godless
deserve healing

for sharing with them
our salt and bread

The Master Gardener's Window

The window is open as I promised.

With the clanging from the bell tower, the pharaoh rats have scuttled away. At this hour the walls of the *alcazaba* are taller, the screech owls are white faced and still. Iberian eagles loop around the fort, tying it in chains. Bats hang like armor. I smell the massacre. It is late.

I smell the massacre, not the lemon groves, the musk roses. The window is open as I promised.

Our books are still smoldering. When the Kufic pieces lay burning, I thought I saw the fire opal of my mother's delicate fingernails in the sparks. So long had she cared for these fragments of my father's calligraphy that they held her essence. Today I saw them burn on the blood-red crown of Granada—Alhamra on the laden Sebeka.

The moon is weak through the filigreed arches. It is late. When Isabella's men come asking, I give them my mother's old name—Antonia. A disguise does not last long with them. I breathe in massacre.

Our maps leapt high for an instance before they burned, as if the wind would steal them from the fire. I watched with the silence of a dead tree. Only when I heard the muffled sobbing I almost shouted I am Aliya not Antonia. It is late, husband. The window is open as I promised you. The almonds you planted, the olives you tended are a darkling vision. Your blooms have all withered. You said you will come if you are alive.

Hear the starling, the fire-crest by the fountain? The morning sky shows itself in a shroud of jacarandas and cypresses.

The Castilian men are ashen as if they feed on the books they burn. The inquisition has plugged our mouths. Listen to the blue magpie, the rustling in the jasmines, the jagged cry of a deaf child.

The Stonemason' Son
Contemplates Death

Because my heart
became a kiln
I wished to die

The inscription on the tiles
made a prayer in butterfly script
crowning your well

May the water refresh your soul

The clanging of keys became loud
A soldier stood behind me pissing in the well

Someone sang in the distance
Couldn't tell if she was a Jew
Christian or Muslim

It was a devotional song

Cleansing

Hysteria brought on by
un-dyed leather *N'ayl*
scattered in the courtyard

Sandals?
How could sandals
drive a man to claw his own cheeks?

They follow him
soundlessly
the smallest ones chase him into nettles

Their wearers had been burned
A whole family of *moriscos*
wrapped in linen and torched
for washing their feet

Window in La Madraza

In the University
Rooms echo with the pounding
One last ache
For any thing that was ever dear

This is how death begins
The soldiers use rope
To tie five or six heavy ones
Ten or twelve light

Years though only a few hundred
This scent of tannin and reed remains
Of the scribe and the reader
Scent of words over and over

And above
The funeral pyre of books
Rise memories of the paper that was linen
Made into pages one at a time

Meaning left in the powder of ash
The soot on the cheeks
Of the soldiers
And the grieving ones

Window Open to Plaza de Bab-Al-Ramla

In its hunger, the fire has crawled to the top so fast that by the time I reach the master he is already a dwarf against the view of the burning wall. The window is thrown open. He seems older now, as if he were part of the dry foliage that frames the window, a lank vine offering itself to the whetted tongues. His prayer beads break and fall on the tiles of the ledge like sudden rain. He does not hear them. He is relieved the burden of sound. Ibn Hazm, the poet, is deaf to the wails of the crowd, to the barking of the soldiers building the wall of books, to the wild ranting fire. When I put my arms around him I fear he might turn to dust. I am not a soldier this instant but the boy from Malaga he had found selling figs in a summer storm, many years ago. My dearest friend, do you remember how you wrote poems on the sloped floor of the patio and I read them once in the morning light and once in the fading light before you would light the lamps? Remember the walnut poem by the poet from Sevilla? I would recite it to olive groves and to sacks of dried figs. Remember how the sun seemed to swim in the Xenil? How I ran away after the beating I got in the village for reciting Moorish poetry? When I said the orchard loves me and the sun swims with me and the breeze carries prayers for me, you said I was a real poet, and that day, I felt like a king. In his eyes I see the imprint of my Castilian tunic and the glacial bones of burned books. He is lifeless. I had come to hand him the poems of the great man he is named after. I wanted to tell him I saved his poet from the fire. He has seen enough. His prayer beads fall off the ledge one by one.

The Fire did not Cool
for the People of Abraham

Loaves of bread
long charred

and obsidian as books
containing the grain
of Maimonides
Averroes
Albucasis

When the spell broke

Ziryab's lute strings
were strewn like intestines of stray animals
Carved wood ceilings had turned
into snuff-boxes

Galleries were sweating paint

On the walnut shelves
Corpses with coins

Groves cut down
to feed a furnace
with unfaithful
innocents

Exile

One crystal jar for saffron
One for sugar
One for tears
I'll watch the last wicked
shower of sand
in the hour-glass
 while the neighbor's boy plays the *oud*
the baby naps here under the jacarandas
and the bread rises
When it is time you pour the honey
of your voice to calm the children
I'll know to fold and fasten
their bedding
And catch the last sun-beams
touching our house

Stopped by Robbers After Leaving Sefarad

Things that my cloak
yielded:
My grandfather's Torah in a sandalwood case
Mother's perfume
 and portrait in a *Keswa Kbira*
of velvet
smoother than your tongue
It had sheer
tea-colored sleeves
ruffled at the edges
embroidered in red with slender
gold oblong buds

And it made me sweat
to think of my father's Toledo
sword

But it did not catch their eye
Hidden deep in the baby's carrier

Sorrows of Moraima

And so she is wed
in her plain *mantilla,*
the stoic *vezir's*
sixteen-year old Moraima
to Abu-abdallah, *rey el chico.*
She has three times as many sorrows as you,
lone cypress with the bent torso!
I watch her burn before she has bloomed.
I, the window they call
the eyes of Ayesha.
I, myself a gaping book waiting to be written,
watch her pace through white corridors,
reading passages between
the hissing walls.
A husband at war, a child taken captive,
all day she digs for a window.
All the while I let in common sparrows,
twigs, pollen, arrows of winter rain,
she is behind deaf *carmen* walls
in the city below
shut away from this, her palace.
Three times your sorrows, broken cypress.

Twelve Hundred Lions

Alone in the *Rauda*, Lady Aisha cups her hand, a beggar for the dirt in the garden of the dead. El Zogoybi's cradle had smelled like this. The phantom odor sucked up the musk and camphor on her skin, spitting out a curse on her palm. The mantle from the land of *sirgo* became a flag, then a sea of mulberries. She sank to the bottom of that purple silk of silence, cocoons shriveling all around her. Anchor appeared in her dreams as the stone mane of the lion in the courtyard. It turned to a chant. Each of the lions of the fountain gave birth, silence jetting out of their slit-throats. She grew wings so long they dipped in the Vega, all for the dirt in the garden of the dead. Flying over Alhamra, she looked for the *mexura*, the court of myrtles, granaries, the royal stables. All charred, except for the garden of the dead. In the scrawny web of ivy on its gate, there were constellations. Among these, the one her child was born under. El Zogoybi, the unfortunate. This is the hour before exile. And the moon shines in the lily pond, the roses cover the mosaic, the stone lions roar without sound, but she will dream only of the garden of the dead. Bones are cradles for memories. Here, the walls have stature; trees give shade, bear fruit, bear fruit.

Window in the Tower of the Seven Floors
Boabdil's Lament

The red sky sent a rain
of keys.

Keys,
sharp and cold and heavy,
fell and fell, their necks unbending.

I told them:

Do not spare Boabdil of the spiked cradle.

I tried to swallow a key at dawn,
the window flanked with my sigh.
I, Boabdil of the bent neck.

The sky fell in a serrated rhythm.
My key and my kingdom
are eaten away.
Isabella of Castile,
take my Alhamra,
but brick up this portal forever.

What had come was lightning
What leaves is a wisp of white hair.

Queen Isabella Enters the Alhamra

The breeze in the lopped off minaret
is the moor's last breath

Stones become crowns
(The moor is not yet cold)
in the pulse of honeycomb
structures

Every day I will fall
in his geometric web of light

And every night try to erase him

this rippled electricity of stars
green clock of the lotus

Silk suturing stone:
"La ghalib illa Allah"

Solo Allah es vencedor

Repeated in one million
ribbons of flickering water

Sultana Moraima Descends the Hill of Sebeka

Wingless in the city
of the falconers

My blood runs through your silk

Granada
Inked pomegranate

Write down this last Cypress walk
to my child
Captive of Alabaster queen

Prince Ahmed Sees
his Wet Nurse
on the Day of his Wedding

You had arrived in half a yard
of Granada silk
The first to go
was the gold prayer bracelet

Windows thrown open
all summer you cried in the servant quarters
The arches beyond
clasping
the moon: a pearl
passed from a forgotten oyster
to forever dangle
like you, niño.

By age seven
even the thoughtful look of your grandfather the vizier
was gone from your eyes.
Sour fruit accent
of your mother's song
gone.

A tutor pressed your voice like a soldier's tunic.
Not a crease of Arabic.
(And God bless you)
No name for father.

Juana La Loca

It's true they say she hung
from her jeweled veil
knotted around a cypress:
A muddy pendulum
swinging away the hours of a fever
Waiting to be snapped by a wind
from Galicia
Chafed by her embroidered under-sleeves

& then she squealed
at the face in the lily pond:
Lovely Isabella
only younger & cracked
& glued back into provinces
& haunted by heads on holy platters
mouths gossamered with prayers

Child-mother
A rooster in her armpit
A knife on her tongue

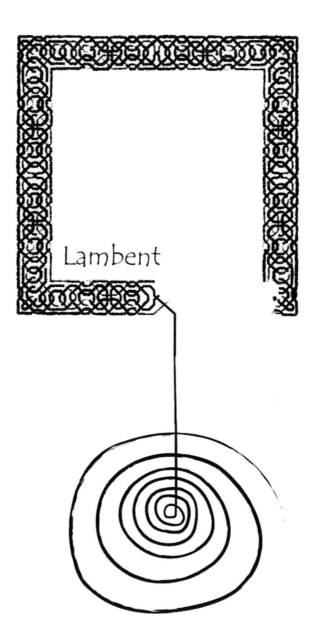

Lambent

Mosaic

The sun's brash mirror
has fissures

Longing
at this latitude
becomes lambent

Piecing together in the middle of the earth

A Mediterranean psalm
tagged to a guitar
        floating you home

Soul in Mezquita Antiqua
(Cordoba: 2003)

There is an abandoned scooter in the narrow street of the
juderia. A dove rests on it. In the milky light, with the traces of
rain only in the scent of the earth, this bird could be the one
Noah sent to find out whether the world was habitable. It stirs
at the sound of school children and hops on to the wall of the
synagogue. The day sweet and filled with light, it glides over
the dome of the mosque. In the patio of oranges, there are
fountains for ablution. It drinks the water, leaves the patio
glistening like a worshipper. There are memories of a nest here.
It flies to the enormous bell of the cathedral in the lungs of the
mosque. Broken feathers float in the gilded emptiness, the
chapel agape, like eternity. There are old songs in the breeze.
The bird is drawn to the balconies of the juderia looking for its
mate. The ground beneath her pulsates with dead worshippers,
the mate's blood still warm on the sacred floor.

Etymology

Achacar is
to blame
in Spanish

comes from Tashakka
in Arabic

Ashk
are tears in Urdu

Sleep-sill Canvas

The windowpanes are membranes, thinly sprawled on the green
　　bones
of the casement. The window must be hundreds of years old. It slams
and swings open, nearly unhinging itself every time. So old,
it opens to the city of Ur, the Yellow river of *Li-sao*,
the great granary of Indus, a *Badhaus*, a sunken garden. So old,
yet, I am certain it is motorized, because all the sepia-hue builders
of the Pyramids, all the ravaging armies of Tamburlane and Xerxes,
could not clamor the way it does. It is powered by a desperate engine
that makes it shudder incessantly. It will tremor but won't come loose,
for its aged sash passes straight through the center of the earth.

I see the window in every sleep-sill, one foot into wakefulness.

I have been running away from a painting.
The canvas, six feet by six feet, stretches and stretches. It will catch up.
But the window I have already painted never emerges.
The jagged window of my dream,
neither drawn inwards nor outwards, goes on thundering.

Wishing a stronger body,
I had painted you
mahogany; rich, impenetrable.

With each brush-stroke, the wood seemed ready and more ready
for the crawling of worms in the rain, for the resting of hill-mynahs
and sand-colored birds in springtime.

The lilac on the glass was my soul,
dusty, vulnerable.
And so, all around the Mahogany skeleton, there had to be a room
looking inwards, using a foot and a half of space. Perhaps,
my black library desk showing. Perhaps,
my hand.
On the six by six canvas:

You showed
a craggy, perfect outer world.

A perfect world through a craggy window: A working form in
silhouette, conical outlines
of butterfly-bush, rosemary and dahlias in a garden.
Not such as that of the dream; the over-grown Eden, with its hissing,
and slithering, its green so deep, I paled and begged for air.
But a garden where terrible mistakes like fear and doubt, avarice
and arrogance, the wish to possess, to live forever, are erased
with but one quick spray. I painted a newly grown garden;
sharp, mystic, responsive,
where peace is what the gazer must bring to it constantly,
like portions of sunshine, rain, manure.

I have been running away from myself; into magma, into ice, into gesso.
The window, six feet by six feet, stretched, damp, smelling of linseed,
has clung like phantom ink to my wall.
A composition in lint, in eel slime.

You
Are Hanging.

You, who are fennel-feeble,
do not instruct me pansies are for thoughts,
and rosemary for remembrance.

Not yet. I must feed you thick coats of paint, obsess you,
robust you with large doses of lightning.

I have paint enough
for a life-time.

Bakery Window in Algeciras

Once there was a door around a knob. A youth stood before it transfixed. An old man turned the knob. He could have been the muleteer with the gold key whose stories of Granada's riches no one believed until the scrolls were found. The knob was a navel leading to the gut of Spain or to a massive oven for rainbow fish. Out here in smoke-filled Algeciras who would believe? This was the noisy embryo, where dreams begin in murmurs, then roars come folded in dust. Of this we had read "forgettable port city," the afternoon sweltering and bitter from the sea. The only word shoveled out of the salt was "desire." In the thin blue air of the port, the anchor is umbilical. See Africa through the fog? The straits pulsate between the continent of fire and the one of ice. Our tea arrives cold. The glass on the bakery window is wide and forbidding as the sea. The old man has opened the door with a knob in its middle and gone in. The youth does not believe it is an actual door.

Return of Happiness

I was dough
Running away in a baker's dream
All honeyed
and rolling the morning

sun into clammy skin

The day was steep and over
Before I made it far
from the oven
Far from the one who chased
Long out of breath

And I hid
Under the concrete
Hid from the ants and the stray cat
until flowers grew out of me

Fool the minutes crawling
The whiskers of time brushing past?

I packed my heart in a clock for you.

Notes

✍ ALCAZAR IN A DREAM
Alcazar: palace.

✍ WINDOW OVERLOOKING THE FURN
Furn: a communal oven.

"In a world torn by religious antagonism, lessons can be
learned from medieval Spanish villages where Muslims,
Christians, and Jews rubbed shoulders on a daily basis—
sharing irrigation canals, bathhouses, municipal ovens, and
marketplaces. Medieval Spaniards introduced Europeans to
paper manufacture, Hindu-Arabic numerals, philosophical
classics, algebra, citrus fruits, cotton, and new medical
techniques. Her mystics penned classics of Kabbalah and
Sufism. More astonishing than Spain's wide-ranging
accomplishments, however, was the simple fact that until the
destruction of the last Muslim Kingdom by King Ferdinand
and Queen Isabella in 1492, Spain's Muslims, Christians, and
Jews often managed to bestow tolerance and freedom of
worship on the minorities in their midst."—Chris Lowney

✍ BAKER OF TARIFA
Tarifa is named after Tarif Bin Malik, the first Muslim to
enter Spain.

✍ THE CONFECTIONER'S DISTRICT IN SEVILLA
The poem is meant for three voices and to be read
horizontally across the columns.

Muslims were the first to plant sugarcane in Europe and to
develop the technology to make and refine sugar.

✍ A SCRIBE IS VISITED BY A JINNI
Jinni is the singular of Jinn or Djinn. In Islamic tradition, the
jinn (literally "hidden" or "concealed") are supernatural
creatures that have a parallel existence with humans. Like
humans and unlike angels, the jinn possess free will.
Comparable to this in the west is the notion of "genius"
(which comes from "genie" or "guardian spirit" in Latin).

Muslim women often worked as scribes. Historian Ibn al-
Fayyad reported that 170 women were engaged as copyists
in only one section of Córdoba alone. The most commonly
used paper in Andalus was made from linen. Paper from
sugarcane pulp was not developed until much later.

EUROPE'S FIRST PALM
Syrian prince and poet Abd-al Rahman planted Europe's
first palm in memory of Rusafa, his home. By establishing the
Umayyad dynasty (755) in Cordoba, Spain, he laid the
foundation for the civilization of Al Andalus. The
distinguishing feature of Al Andalus is the sustaining of a
peaceful co-existence between Jews, Christians and Muslims
through most of the eight hundred years of its history.
Between periods of unprecedented intellectual, artistic and
scientific achievements were periods of war and bitterness.
Al Andalus's final collapse came with the Inquisition and
Reconquista in 1492.

MY HUSBAND BRINGS A POET'S RABAB FROM ABROAD
First bowed instrument brought into the West, the rabab
originated in Persia and is said to be the precursor to
instruments like the violin. Historians are not sure if the
poet's rabab ("rabab al shair") which has a single string,
entered Andalusi culture. Other kinds of rababs were
common.

A HALVA VENDOR REMEMBERS
Andalusia developed a distinct script of Arabic calligraphy
that was used for books and buildings as well as artifacts
made out of ceramic, leather, wood, cloth, ivory and other
materials. The verse ("but the doves laughed") is by Al
Marini, a 12th century poet.

MARZIPAN ROSES
"According to Gregorio Maranon, the closed religious orders
preserved the craft of making marzipan through the thick
and thin of history. Convents took up making sweets as a
source of income, to survive, and continued using and
perfecting their antique recipes through the centuries.
Indeed, Maranon points out, sweets such as marzipan have
become symbols of the complex heritage of the Spanish
people." —Tor Eigland

WALLADA'S LAST POEM FOR IBN ZAYDUN
Wallada (1011-1091) and Ibn Zaydun (1003-1071) were
famous poets of Umayyad Spain. The sculpture of the hands
of Wallada and Ibn Zaydun was placed in the plaza El
Campo Santo de los Martires in 1971.

A GAME OF SIX, DEUCE AND ACE
King Alfonso X (1221—1284) of Castile, Leon and Galicia

commissioned an illustrated work called the *Book of Games*.
It includes games such as Chess, "Six, Deuce and Ace" or
Backgammon, and a version of "Tic, Tac, Toe" — all which
came to Europe via Spain. Historian Al Masudi wrote about
(956 CE) these board games played by men, women and
children in the Muslim world.

✍ DIVORCE

Poet, historian and theologian Ibn Hazm wrote the famous
Tawq al Hamama or the "Dove's Neck Ring" in his youth and
revised it later. It is a literary classic and is known for its
penetrating insight into human psychology. According to
him "true love is a spiritual approbation, a fusion of souls."

✍ YUSUF POEMS

In the Abrahamic tradition, Yosef, Joseph or Yusuf had been
bestowed with the gift of interpreting dreams.

✍ YUSUF REMEMBER'S HIS FATHER'S DONKEY

Maristan: Hospital

✍ YUSUF SEES THE GHOST OF THE LAST QUEEN OF AL ANDALUS

Eid: An Islamic holiday following *Ramadan*, the month of
fasting. It is customary to celebrate by wearing new clothes.
During the Inquisition period, it was a punishable offense to
wear new clothes on Eid day.

Moraima, the last queen of Al Andalus died soon after
Granada fell. Her bereaved husband secretly carried her
corpse from Andarax to Monduja (to be buried with other
members of the family) and furnished that mosque with
funds. According to Fidel Fernández—"Just after Boabdil's
departure for his exile in Morocco, the Christians seized the
properties designed for the prayers in favor of Moraima and
built a church with them upon the premises of a mosque,
which they had previously demolished." The persecution of
Muslims by Christians began around this time.

✍ WINDOW FOR FOUR VOICES

The poem is read horizontally across the columns.

✍ WINDOW OF THE ORATORY

Sultan Al Ahmer aligned himself with King Ferdinand III,
making Granada a tributary state. A peace-loving man,
Ahmer fought against Sevilla (1248) on behalf of Ferdinand

and was said to have grieved later. He built the Alhamra palace and founded the longest lasting Muslim dynasty to rule in Spain.

✍   PLAGUE PRAYERS
The deadly outbreak of the Bubonic Plague in 14th century Europe caused severe religious intolerance. The plague was thought to be a form of divine punishment for co-mingling with "non- believers."

✍   THE MASTER GARDENER'S WINDOW
The inquisition sought to remove all traces of Al Andalus.

✍   CLEANSING
Ablutions before the Muslim prayer requires the washing of feet. The *moriscos* or Muslim converts to Catholicism were punished for lapsing into their original faith. An act suggesting the practice of Islam by the *moriscos* was an offense punishable by a heavy fine, torture or even death. "The chief business of the inquisition was the searching out and punishing of false *conversos*. This was done with a persistence, thoroughness and heartlessness that shocked Pope Sixtus IV himself."—Henry Lea

✍   WINDOW IN LA MADRAZA
In 1499, the famous library of Muslim Granada housed in La Madraza was burned by the orders of Cardinal Cisneros who used the building later for carrying out the operations of the Inquisition.

✍   WINDOW OPEN TO PLAZA DE BAB-AL-RAMLA
Muslim Granadans were forced to watch the burning of their books. Some Christian soldiers secretly tried to save some of these books.

✍   THE FIRE DID NOT COOL FOR THE PEOPLE OF ABRAHAM
In the Islamic tradition, King Namrud tried to kill prophet Ibrahim (Abraham) but God would not allow him to perish. To safeguard Ibrahim, God made the logs in the fire sprout forth a garden of fruit, and a well "which bubbled fresh water from Paradise."

"All the worst features of the medieval inquisition were to be found in the Spanish Inquisition. It operated secretly, the accusers were not given the names of the accused; torture was used to obtain confessions; those convicted were subject to confiscation of property for the benefit of the state, as well as exile, imprisonment, or burning at the stake"—Joseph F. O'Callaghan

Maimonides or Rabbi Moshe Ben Maimon (1135—1204) was a native Cordoban where he was trained as a physician. During the intolerant rule of the Almohades, he moved to Fez where he was recognized for his brilliance. He became the court physician to the grand Vizier Alfadil and then to Sultan Salahuddin (Saladin). Maimonides is thought to be one of the most influential figures in medieval Jewish philosophy. A popular medieval saying that also served as his epitaph states, From Moshe (of the Torah) to Moshe (Maimonides) there was none like Moshe.

Averroes or Ibn Rushd (1126—1198) has been described as "the founding father of secular thought in Europe." He was a master of Islamic philosophy, mathematics, theology, Arabic music theory, psychology, and the sciences of medicine, astronomy and physics.

Albucasis or Abu'l Qasim al Zahrawi is known as the father of modern surgery. He authored the work *Kitab al Tasrif*,which is known in the west as *Concessio*, and is a medical encyclopedia (in 30 volumes) covering orthopedics, ophthalmology, pharmacology, dentistry, gynecology and nutrition besides surgery. He served as court physician to Al Hakam II.

✍   EXILE
In 1492, the Jews who had called Spain home for centuries ("since the time of the prophets") were exiled by the Catholic monarchs Isabella and Ferdinand. This was followed by the exile, forced conversion and genocide of Spanish Muslims.

✍   STOPPED BY ROBBERS AFTER LEAVING SEFARAD
Sefarad: Ancient Jewish name for Spain.

✍   SORROWS OF MORAIMA
Soon after her marriage to the Nasrid prince Abu Abdullah (known as Boabdil and Rey El Chico in the West), Sultana Moraima was imprisoned. Her two sons were taken away from her in infancy by the Castilian royal family and were raised Catholic.

✍ TWELVE HUNDRED LIONS

Sultana Aisha La Hora was the mother of the last king of Muslim Spain (Granada) Abu Abdullah (Boabdil) also known as El Zogoybi or "the unfortunate one." Despite Aisha's courage in the face of calamity, Granada fell to the Catholic Monarchs, after a ten-year war. Exiled, she died in Africa.

✍ WINDOW IN THE TOWER OF THE SEVEN FLOORS

The prosperous and highly developed civilization of Al Andalus, the pre-cursor to European Renaissance, came to an end in 1492 with the Nasrid dynasty, the last to rule Muslim Spain which had, by then, diminished only to Granada.

✍ QUEEN ISABELLA ENTERS THE ALHAMRA

Isabella has been described as "beautiful and pious." She was dressed in Andalusi attire the day she took the keys of the Alhamra from Boabdil.

"And yet, for all this brutal persecution of the Moriscos (Moors) there is indisputable evidence of a deep respect among the Christians for the Islamic culture they were publicly trying to negate."—Michael Jacobs, *Alhambra*

✍ SULTANA MORAIMA DESCENDS THE HILL OF SEBEKA

On the day the keys of the Alhamra were surrendered to the new Catholic rulers, Moraima's son Ahmed, nicknamed "*infantico*" by Queen Isabella, was to be returned to the Nasrid family. Most sources say he never was.

✍ PRINCE AHMED SEES HIS WET NURSE ON THE DAY OF HIS WEDDING

Born in 1483, Moraima's son Ahmed ("infantico") was raised by the servants of the Catholic monarchs.

✍ JUANA LA LOCA

Juana La Loca (1479-1555) was the daughter of Isabella and Ferdinand. She had acute manic depression and was locked up in a windowless prison for fifty years by her husband Phillip and by her son Carlos V.

Biography

Shadab Zeest Hashmi has an MFA from Warren Wilson. She graduated from Reed College in 1995. She has been on the editorial board of *The Poetry Conspiracy*. She has also been the editor of the annual *Magee Park Poet's Anthology* since 2000. Originally from Pakistan, she lives in San Diego, California.

Lightning Source UK Ltd.
Milton Keynes UK
UKOW04f1201201115

263101UK00002B/19/P